MW00697360

WHAT HAPPENS WHEN

Parents Get Divorced

Advocacy Resource Center
Serving Survivors Since 1989
(906)632-1808
Toll Free (877)639-7820

written + illustrated by
SARA OLSHER

mighty ᴬᴺᴰ bright™

helping families handle hard things

Hi, my name is Mia!

And this is Stuart.
Stuart feels better when he knows
what's going to happen every day.

(Actually, *everybody* feels better when they know
what's going to happen—even grown-ups!)

Most of the time,
we do the same things in the mornings.
We wake up.

We eat breakfast.
(I like apples. Stuart only eats bugs.)

Usually our nights are the same too.
We brush our teeth.

We put on our jammies, and we go to bed.
Every day ends with sleep.

But our days can be different.

Some days we go to school,
and some days are the weekend!

When something big changes,
what we do each day can change too.
Stuart wants to know what happens to our days
when our parents get a **divorce**.

But he doesn't really understand what divorce is.
Do you?

Divorce is when parents decide
not to be married anymore,
and they live in two different houses.

Hearing this makes Stuart upset.
He wants to know
what's going to happen.
What about me?

At first, divorce can be confusing or scary for kids.
After all, you can't be in two houses at the same time.

Some kids worry that they caused their parents to get a divorce,
especially if the parents argue about the kids.

Kids making mistakes is not why parents get divorced.
Divorce is never, ever a kid's fault.
Divorce is *always* about the parents' problems with each other,
but *never* about their problems with their kids.

When parents divorce, they usually move into two different houses, and things change for everyone in the family.

Or a treehouse?

...what about me? Where do I go?

Sometimes each parent gets a new place to live, and sometimes only one does.

The kids spend some of the time at one house and some of the time at the other house.

Some kids spend the same amount of time with each parent.
Other kids live with one parent most of the time and visit the other parent.
Every family is different.

Your parents can use a calendar
to show you when you'll see each parent.

Some days, you go to sleep
in the same house you wake up in.
Other days, you might wake up at one house
and go to sleep at the other house.

Divorce might make you feel some really big feelings.
You might get angry or sad or worried because it's different now,
and you're wondering if it's different *good* or different *bad*.

It might be a little bit of both.

There are some good things about divorce.
First, after a divorce, parents do not fight as much,
which means they're happier and can be more fun to be around.

Two houses also means that kids get two bedrooms, two sets of toys,
and even two toothbrushes, which can be fun!

There are also some not-so-great things about divorce.

When you are with one parent, you might miss your other parent. When this happens, come up with a plan for when you can talk to them on the phone or see their face. You can also look at your calendar for when you'll see them next.

Another not-very-fun thing about divorce is that sometimes parents don't get along. Sometimes they get mad at each other and can't agree on things.

That can be hard for kids. Sometimes you might feel like you're in the middle, which is no fun at all.

Everyone—including your parents—hopes that will change.
It might take a while for them to get along, but hopefully they can
remember to be kind to each other.

The longer parents are divorced,
the easier it is for them to get along.

The family is going through something hard right now,
but it *will* get so much easier.

Unfortunately, there is nothing you can do to fix your parents' marriage.
You didn't cause the divorce (that's impossible), and you can't stop it either.

For a while, it might feel like your family is broken.
But it's not broken—it's just different now.
And there is one very important thing to remember:

Even if your parents don't love each other the same way anymore,
they will always love *you*. A parent's love for their kids is *forever*.

Some kids worry about their parents and want to make sure they are okay.
But grown-ups are grown up! It's their job
to take care of their feelings *and* help you with yours.

Even though some things are changing,
lots of things will stay the same.

Every morning, you will wake up, and every night, you'll go to sleep.
Your parents will always be your parents, and they will always love you.

Stuart feels a lot better now that he knows what to expect.
Even though our days can be different, it helps to plan out
our week together so we know what's going to happen next.

There are a lot of fun things to look forward to,
like movie nights, sports, play dates, craft time,
and special time with each parent.

And remember, when things get hard, it's important to share how you are feeling with a grown-up.

By planning special time together, you have a time when you know it's okay to talk about your feelings ... or anything else! *We can do hard things together!*

And don't forget, Stuart... even the biggest feelings don't last forever.

Hi! My name is Sara, and I write + illustrate kids' books.

I wrote this book (and 6 others!) because I like to draw + help people.

Things I LOVE!

reading
Dancing (Badly)
my Family
nature
our dog, Honey
candy
Rainbows
Quiet time

I live in California where they make wine out of grapes.

I do all my drawings on an iPad with an Apple pencil

I live with my daughter, my partner, his daughter, and our dog. I want a goat, and I want to name him **CAULIFLOWER!**

my books come with fun calendars just for kids, because...

Knowing what to expect makes divorce way easier.

(actually life is _always_ easier when you know what happens next!)

Know when you will see each parent

Plan your mornings & afternoons

see which day you will switch houses

find them at mightyandbright.com!
(along with loads of other helpful stuff!)

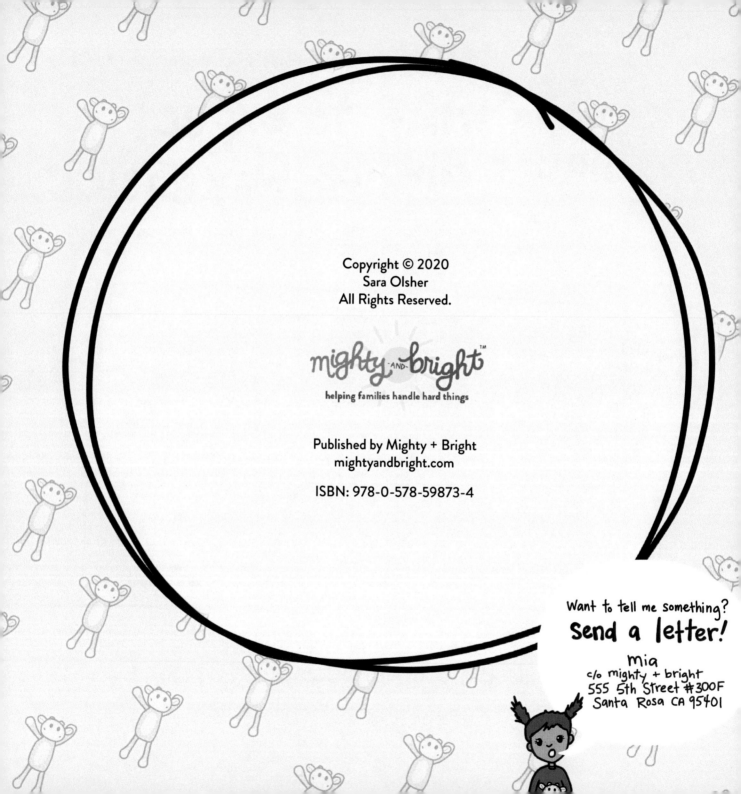

Copyright © 2020
Sara Olsher
All Rights Reserved.

mighty -AND- bright™

helping families handle hard things

Published by Mighty + Bright
mightyandbright.com

ISBN: 978-0-578-59873-4

Want to tell me something?
send a letter!
mia
c/o mighty + bright
555 5th Street #300F
Santa Rosa CA 95401

Made in the USA
Middletown, DE
09 December 2021

54929605R00018